M000191547

Dear Mom

Dear Mom

A journal all about US written by ME

Kate Fox

spruce

An Hachette UK Company
www.hachette.co.uk

First published in Great Britain in 2014 by
Spruce, a division of Octopus Publishing Group Ltd,
Endeavour House, 189 Shaftesbury Avenue, London,
WC2H 8JY
www.octopusbooksusa.com

Copyright © Octopus Publishing Group Ltd 2014

Distributed in the US by Hachette Book Group USA,
237 Park Avenue, New York, NY 10017, USA

Distributed in Canada by Canadian Manda Group,
165 Dufferin Street, Toronto, Ontario, Canada
M6K 3H6

All rights reserved. No part of this work may
be reproduced or utilized in any form or by any means,
electronic or mechanical, including photocopying,
recording or by any information storage and retrieval
system, without the prior written permission of the
publisher.

Kate Fox asserts the moral right to be identified
as the author of this work

ISBN 978 1 84601 469 7

Printed and bound in China

10 9 8 7 6 5 4 3 2 1

Consultant Publisher: Sarah Ford
Designer: Eoghan O'Brien
Copy-editor: Jane Birch
Production Controller: Sarah Connelly
Illustrations: Kath/KJA artists

To all our moms

Contents

All that I am, or hope to be, I owe to my mother.

Abraham Lincoln

Introduction

From your first breath of life to your high school graduation, from your first hesitant baby steps to your radiant walk down the aisle, your mom is with you for all your major milestones and all the parts in between, too. Your relationship with your mother is one of the most important constants in your life. The very special woman who gave birth to you and cared for you during your first years of life has never stopped caring since. But, such is the incredible everlasting love your mom provides, it can be easy to take this bond of love and respect for granted—and sometimes we can forget just how remarkable our mothers are.

This an opportunity for you to revisit and reveal your heartfelt feelings for your mother in a keepsake that will last a lifetime. Using thoughtful prompts to help you organize your feelings, it is the perfect way to look at your relationship through new eyes, and articulate your unconditional love for your mom.

Show your mom what she really means to you, how she has shaped your life and made you the person you are today, and what lasting memories of her you have kept closest to your heart. With spaces to put in treasured photos, this will be a lasting reminder of how much she really means to you.

insert a photo of you as a child here

My mother had a great deal of trouble with me, but I think she enjoyed it.

Mark Twain

Chapter One

About Me

My given name:

....

The name I like to go by:

....

I was born in:

....

I live in:

....

My birthday:

....

My astrological sign:

....

My current age:

....

My eye color:

....

The color of my hair:

....

insert a photo of you and your siblings here

I have.....................brothers and....................sisters

Having siblings is:

....
....
....
....

Not having siblings is:

....
....
....

I sometimes wished for:

···
···
···

Growing up in a family this size taught me:

···
···
···
···

What I treasure about being the oldest/youngest/middle/only child is

···
···
···
···

I sometimes find it hard being the oldest/youngest/middle/only child because:

···
···
···

A favorite family saying is:

···
···

My best friend is:

....

I like...................because:

....

....

We met...................ago at:

....

Three words I would use to describe him/her are:

....

The one thing I will never forget about him/her is:

....

Another close friend is:

....

I like.....................because:

....

....

We met...................ago at:

....

....

insert a photo of you and your friend(s) here

Here I am with:

....

....

I love my friends because:

....

....

....

....

....

....

....

....

....

The places my friends and I like to go are:

....

....

....

When we hang out we like to:

....

....

....

....

My friends really helped me out when:

....

....

....

....

....

....

I was able to help my friends out when:

....

....

....

....

....

....

The food I like best is:

....

My favorite drink is:

....

My favorite fruit is:

....

The breakfast I enjoy most is:

....

My least favorite food is:

....

because:

....
....
....

My least favorite drink is:

....

because:

....
....

Three places where I love to eat out are:

....
....
....

My favorite take-out is:

....

I wish I liked .... because:

....
....

If I had to give up any food forever it would be:

....

because:

....
....
....

I love/don't like to cook because:

....
....
....
....
....

I like music that makes me feel:

....

....

My favorite male artist is:

....

I think his best song is:

....

My favorite female artist is:

....

My favorite song of hers is:

....

My favorite band is:

....

And my favorite song of theirs is:

....

because:

....

....

....

I would love to see .... live in concert

because:

....
....
....

I would love to learn to play the:

....

If I were in a band, it would be called:

....

A song I love singing is:

....

because:

....
....
....

I first heard it:

....
....
....
....

The sport I like to play is:

....

because:

....

My favorite sport to watch is:

....

because:

....

....

The sport team I support is:

....

My favorite professional athlete is:

....

An extreme sport I wish I could try is:

....

The sport I least like watching is:

....

....

....

My favorite TV show is:

....

because:

....
....

The three TV celebrities I like most are:

....
....
....

My favorite movie is:

....

because:

....
....

My all-time favorite movie stars are:

....
....

If I could star in any film or TV show, it would be:

....
....

The book I love most is:

....

because:

....

....

The magazine I read most often is:

....

My favorite poem is:

....

My favorite artist is:

....

because:

....

....

The flower I love best is the:

....

because:

....

....

insert a photo of an object you have collected here

My favorite word is:

....

My favorite color is:

....

For me,................is the best part of the day

I like to collect:

....
....
....
....

One thing I've always wanted to try is:

....

....

My favorite season is:

....

What I love most about it is:

....

....

....

My idea of perfect relaxation is:

....

....

....

....

When I need space to think I like to go to:

....

....

It helps me to clear my head because:

....

....

....

The man who really inspires me is:

....

He is an inspiration because:

....
....
....
....
....
....
....

The woman I find truly inspirational is:

....

She is an inspiration to me because:

....
....
....
....
....
....
....
....
....
....

If I had three wishes, they would be:

....

....

....

....

....

....

....

The greatest idea I ever had was:

....

....

....

....

A cause I really care strongly about is:

....

....

because:

....

....

....

....

....

....

en things that make me smile are:

. . . .

. . . .

. . . .

. . . .

. . . .

. . . .

. . . .

. . . .

. . . .

. . . .

he most beautiful thing I have ever seen was:

. . . .

. . . .

. . . .

f I could travel anywhere in the world I would choose:

. . . .

ecause:

. . . .

. . . .

. . . .

. . . .

. . . .

The career I have chosen is:

....

I chose this path because:

....
....
....
....
....
....
....
....
....

insert a recent photo of yourself here

The things I think are most important in life are:

....
....
....
....
....
....
....
....
....
....
....
....
....
....
....
....
....
....
....
....
....
....
....
....
....
....

insert a photo of you and your mom here

A mother's arms are made
of tenderness and children
sleep soundly in them.

Victor Hugo

Chapter Two

Memories of Us

When I was younger my favorite thing for us to do together was:

....
....

When I was on my own, I liked to:

....
....

A game I used to really love playing with you was:

....
....
....

I remember that we always had to make time for:

....
....
....

I loved it when you and I:

....
....
....
....
....
....

got upset when:

....
....
....

remember when we had an argument we would make up by:

....
....

One thing that used to really frighten me was:

....

because:

....
....
....

My special household chore was to:

....
....

The pet I really loved was:

....

A pet I always wanted to have was:

....

The toy I loved the most was:

....

I always wanted to be a......................when I grew up

I used to make believe that:

....
....
....

I always wanted to spend my allowance on:

....
....

My favorite Halloween costume was:

....

My favorite party outfit was:

....

The shoes I loved the most were:

....

I really enjoyed dressing up in your:

....
....

My favorite cartoon character was:

....

The TV show I loved to watch with you was:

....

The first book I ever read was:

....

My favorite storybook for you to read aloud to me was:

....

The best story you ever made up for me was:

....
....
....
....

I loved it because:

....
....
....
....
....
....
....

When you used to put me to bed, I remember:

....
....
....
....
....
....
....
....
....
....

The song that you used to sing to me was:

....

The thing I remember most about my bedroom was:

....
....
....

In the mornings we would:

....
....
....
....
....

insert a photo of you at an early age, with your mom, here

One early memory is:

....
....
....

I remember it now because:

....
....
....

Another early memory is the time we:

....
....

I remember getting lost once in:

....

But in the end it was ok because:

....
....
....
....

I used to have bad dreams about:

....
....
....

You would help me by:

....
....
....

I hurt myself once when I:

....
....

You made me feel better by:

....
....

remember you teaching me to:

....
....

really enjoyed learning how to:

....
....

found it really difficult learning how to:

....
....

But in the end you helped by:

....
....

My proudest moment was:

....
....

My most embarrassing moment has to be:

....

But you helped me deal with it by:

....
....

One time that I really got in trouble with you was:

....

....

I remember that you disciplined me by:

....

....

....

I thought it was unfair because:

....

....

But now I can see that:

....

....

....

The one time that I got somebody else into trouble was:

....

....

It made me feel:

....

....

....

The three things that everyone says about dad are:

....
....
....
....
....
....

When I was growing up, what I remember most about dad was:

....
....
....
....
....
....

My favorite thing to do with dad was:

....
....
....

I remember dad always telling me that:

....
....
....
....

As a family, we would sometimes go to:

....

These trips would make me feel:

....

because:

....
....
....

A memory I have of one of these trips is:

....
....
....
....
....

Other places we used to visit as a family were:

....
....
....

My favorite was:

....
....

insert a photo from a family vacation here

The first family vacation I remember was:

....

was....................years old

My favorite memory from this vacation was:

....

Seeing you on vacation, away from home, made me feel:

....

....

....

The things I liked best about being on vacation were:

....

....

....

....

....

The best family vacation we have ever had was:

....

....

....

....

I really loved it because:

....

....

....

....

....

I remember that we bought:

....

....

....

....

....

insert a photo from a family festive holiday here

My favorite festive holiday was:

....

....

I enjoyed helping you to:

....

....

....

The family traditions I enjoyed were:

....

....

....

....

The food that I remember was:

....
....
....
....

The relative I loved to visit most was:

....

because:

....
....
....

A gift I remember receiving was:

....
....
....

The first gift I remember giving you was:

....
....
....
....

insert a school photo here

On my first day of school, I felt:

....

....

....

....

....

....

....

....

....

....

....

....

....

I remember that you:

....

....

When I got home from that first day, I:

....

....

....

The first friend I made was:

....

He/She was:

....

....

We stayed friends for:

....

My teacher was:

....

I loved/hated/didn't mind him/her because:

....

....

....

My favorite class was:

....

because:

....
....

My least favorite class was:

....

because:

....
....

My favorite thing to do at recess was:

....
....
....

In the playground, I loved to play:

....
....

For lunch, I mostly ate:

....
....

insert your favorite photo of your mom here

Mother——that was the bank where we deposited all our hurts and worries.

T. DeWitt Talmag

Chapter Three

About You

Ten words that describe you are:

....
....
....
....
....
....
....
....
....
....

My very earliest memory of you is:

....
....
....
....
....
....
....
....
....
....
....
....
....

One of your favorite things to do when you want to relax is:

....

....

The things that make you happy are:

....

....

....

The three things you least enjoy doing are:

....

....

....

You have a special talent for:

....

....

....

....

A great nickname for you would be:

....

because:

....

....

Your job is:

....

What I admire about your work is:

....
....
....

If I had to do your job, I would:

....
....
....
....

I think you would make a great:

....

because:

....
....
....
....
....
....
....
....

What I have learnt from how you deal with challenges is:

....

....

....

....

....

....

You have always worked hard to provide us with:

....

....

....

....

....

....

Your career choices inspired me to:

....

....

....

....

....

....

....

....

....

insert a photo of your mom dressed for a special occasion here

Three words that describe the way you dress are:

....

....

....

You love to wear:

....

....

....

....

The colors you like best are:

....

....

One item of your clothing I would definitely wear is:

....
....
....

One day I would love to cherish your:

....

When it comes to jewelry, you choose:

....
....

Our taste in clothes is different in these ways:

....
....

The one time you looked amazing was:

....
....
....
....
....
....
....
....
....

The celebrity you most resemble is:

....

because

....
....
....

Your best feature is your:

....
....
....

I love your hair best when:

....
....
....

I'd describe your make-up style as:

....
....

The best style advice you ever gave me was:

....
....
....

ou are one of the best people in the world at:

....
....
....

think you see .... as a priority in life

)ne thing that people always notice about you is:

....
....
....
....

have always wished that I had your:

....
....
....
....

)ne thing you can always forgive is:

....
....

)ne thing you can't stand in people is:

....
....

When I see you and *your* mom together, I think:

. . . .

. . . .

. . . .

. . . .

. . . .

. . . .

. . . .

. . . .

. . . .

I would describe our family as:

. . . .

. . . .

. . . .

. . . .

. . . .

. . . .

. . . .

. . . .

. . . .

. . . .

. . . .

. . . .

. . . .

One achievement you must be so proud of is:

....
....
....
....

One goal you should never give up on is:

....
....
....
....

The saddest I have ever seen you was when:

....
....
....
....

The happiest I have ever seen you was when:

....
....
....

Your favorite quotation is:

....
....

insert a photo of your mom as a child here

When I think of you as a child, I imagine you being:

....

....

I bet you loved to:

....

....

....

....

bet you didn't like:

....
....
....
....
....
....

imagine that you were really good at:

....
....

think you would have got into trouble when:

....
....
....
....

ou were probably best at these games:

....
....
....

ecause:

....
....

The two dishes you cook that I love are:

....

....

I love them because:

....

....

....

I wish that you would make .... more often

The taste of .... always reminds me of home

The best comfort food you ever made me was:

....

....

....

It made me feel better because:

....

....

....

The best birthday cake you ever made me was:

....

....

One kitchen disaster you would never have is:

....

....

When giving gifts you always:

....

....

....

When you receive a gift you always:

....

....

....

If you had three wishes I think that they would be:

....

....

....

....

....

....

If you won the lottery, I think that you would:

....

....

....

insert a favorite photo of you and your mom here

My mother taught me about the power of inspiration and courage, and she did it with a strength and a passion that I wish could be bottled.

Carly Fiorina

Chapter Four

You and Me

The most special thing about our relationship is:

....
....
....
....
....
....
....
....
....
....

When I look in the mirror, I see these features of you in me:

....
....
....
....
....
....
....
....
....
....
....
....

You and I are similar in these ways:

....

....

....

....

....

....

We are totally different in these ways:

....

....

....

....

....

....

Three things you love that I don't are:

....

....

....

....

....

....

....

....

....

The five things I will always be grateful that you taught me are:

....

....

....

....

....

....

....

....

....

....

My favorite thing for us to do together is:

....

....

....

....

....

I love it because:

....

....

....

....

....

....

If I had all the money in the world, I would take you to:

....

because:

....
....
....

The place I've been to, that I'd most like to take you to is:

....

because:

....
....
....
....

A place that we have visited together, that I would love to return to, is:

....

because:

....
....
....
....
....

Our days together are special because:

....
....
....
....
....
....
....
....
....
....

The thing I admire most about you is:

....
....
....
....
....
....
....
....
....
....
....
....

One event that really changed the way I saw you was:

....
....

It made me realize that:

....
....
....

One of the most special moments we've shared together is:

....
....
....
....
....
....
....
....
....
....

I don't ever want to forget the time that you:

....
....
....
....

If I could give you any gift, it would be:

....
....
....

because:

....
....

If we could visit any person, living or dead, together, that person would be:

....

I think you would enjoy it because:

....
....
....
....

I would love it because:

....
....
....
....
....
....

It really makes me laugh when you:

....
....
....
....
....

I think we share a sense of humor in these ways:

....
....
....
....
....

Your favorite joke is:

....
....
....

Mine is:

....
....
....
....
....
....

The goofiest thing that you've ever done has to be:

....

....

....

....

I love to cheer you up by:

....

....

....

....

Something fun that you do often is:

....

....

....

....

One thing that you really don't find funny is:

....

....

....

....

....

....

....

Three things I want from a relationship are:

....
....
....
....
....
....

Your relationship with dad has taught me that:

....
....
....
....
....
....

The things I admire about the way you are together are:

....
....
....
....
....
....
....
....
....

The biggest challenge I've seen you face as parents is:

....

....

....

....

And you came through it because:

....

....

....

....

....

....

I have learned from you that a loving relationship should be:

....

....

....

....

....

....

....

....

....

....

....

One of the hardest things about being a mom is:

....
....
....
....
....
....
....
....
....
....

You deal with this by:

....
....
....
....
....
....
....
....
....
....
....
....

The most important thing that you have taught me about myself is:

....
....
....
....
....
....
....
....
....

The most important thing that I have learned about you is:

....
....
....
....
....
....
....
....
....
....
....
....
....

The life lessons that you have taught me are:

....
....
....
....
....
....
....
....
....
....

You have impacted on my sense of right and wrong because:

....
....
....
....
....
....
....
....
....
....
....
....
....

The dreams that you have inspired me to follow are:

....
....
....
....
....
....
....
....
....
....

You have taught me not to be afraid of:

....
....
....
....
....
....
....
....
....
....
....
....
....

am a stronger person because you:

....
....
....
....
....
....
....
....
....
....

Because of you, my priorities in life are:

....
....
....
....
....
....
....
....
....
....
....
....

When life is tough, I remember that you:

....
....
....
....
....
....
....
....
....
....

I always think of you when:

....
....
....
....
....
....
....
....
....
....
....
....

insert a photo of your family here

The way that you raised our family taught me that:

....

....

....

....

I am/will be ready to raise my own family because of your:

....

....

....

....

....

I have/would like to have...................... girls

I have/would like to have...................... boys

I have named/would like to name my children:

....

....

The pets we have/would like to have are:

....

....

I think the secret to a happy home is:

....

....

....

....

....

....

A cherished family tradition from my childhood that I have
shared/plan to share with my family is:

....

....

....

....

Now I am a parent/If I become a parent, I would like to be like you in these ways:

....

....

....

....

....

....

....

....

....

....

Though I think I will be different in these ways:

....

....

....

....

....

....

....

....

....

....

....

I hope I can be like dad in these ways:

....
....
....
....
....
....
....
....
....

Though I think I will be different in these ways:

....
....
....
....
....
....
....
....
....
....
....
....
....

rom you, I have learned that children are:

....
....
....
....
....
....
....
....
....

Some words of wisdom you told me that I want to pass onto my
children are:

....
....
....
....
....
....
....
....
....
....
....
....

As a grandmother, I think you are/will be:

· ·

· ·

· ·

· ·

· ·

· ·

· ·

· ·

· ·

· ·

· ·

My kids love/would love spending time with you because:

· ·

· ·

· ·

· ·

· ·

· ·

· ·

· ·

· ·

· ·

· ·

insert a photo of your mom with her grandchildren here

I can see you teaching them:

....

....

....

I can see you treating them to:

....

....

....

What my kids love/will love about you is:

....

....

....

I hope that as I grow older, I gain these qualities of yours:

....
....
....
....
....
....
....
....
....
....

The best thing about moms is:

....
....
....
....
....
....
....
....
....
....
....
....
....
....

Something I have always wanted to tell you but have never had the courage to is:

....
....
....
....
....
....
....
....
....
....
....
....
....
....
....
....
....
....
....
....
....
....
....
....